COREY SEEMILLER
MEGHAN GRACE

GENERATION Z
LEADS

**A Guide for Developing the Leadership Capacity of
Generation Z Students**

ISBN: 1456420259
ISBN 13: 9781456420253
Library of Congress Control Number: 2017909361
CreateSpace Independent Publishing Platform
North Charleston, South Carolina

CONTENTS

ABOUT THE AUTHORS

COREY SEEMILLER is a faculty member at Wright State University in the Department of Leadership Studies in Education and Organizations. Her extensive background in both student affairs and instruction in the areas of leadership development, civic engagement, social justice, student success, and career services has offered her insight into working with college students. Corey earned her PhD in higher education from the University of Arizona, is the author of *The Student Leadership Competencies Guidebook* and associated tools and resources, and is coauthor of *Generation Z Goes to College*.

MEGHAN GRACE is an associate with Plaid, LLC. She has served in both campus-based and organizational roles in the areas of leadership development, program and event planning, and fraternity and sorority programs. Meghan earned her Master of Arts degree in higher education from the University of Arizona. She is the coauthor of *Generation Z Goes to College*.

ACKNOWLEDGMENTS

We are incredibly grateful to the reviewers who gave valuable feedback to us in the writing process. A huge thank-you to:

Kathy Guthrie, who serves as an associate professor of higher education in the Department of Educational Leadership and Policy Studies, director of the Leadership Learning Research Center, and coordinator of the Undergraduate Certificate in Leadership Studies at Florida State University. Dr. Guthrie also serves as the associate editor for the New Directions for Student Leadership series and editor of the Contemporary Perspectives in Leadership Learning book series.

Bill Smedick, who serves as a senior lecturer in the Center for Leadership Education at Johns Hopkins University, teaching courses in Leadership Theory, Leading for Social Change, Leading Change, and Leading in Teams. Bill has served as chairperson of the Board of Directors for the National Association for Campus Activities, member of the Board of

Directors for the Council for the Advancement of Standards in Higher Education, and member of the Board of Directors for Lead365.

Josie Alquist, who serves as a national speaker, having trained thousands of student leaders and student affairs professionals on digital leadership. Dr. Alquist has served on the American College Personnel Association President's Task Force on Digital Technology, having chaired the Research and Scholarship team. In 2014 and 2015, Dr. Alquist was named to the "Top 50 Must Read Higher Education Technology Blogs" by Ed Tech.

Susan Luchey, who serves as the associate director of Student Centers for Student Leadership Development at the University of Delaware, overseeing the award-winning Blue Hen Leadership Program. Susan has been recognized by NASPA as a leader in innovative practices for the leadership programs she has created, and the University of Delaware's Student Life Division honored her with a Bright Initiatives Award for her Crucial Conversations program. Susan has also served on the Board of Directors for Lead365 and the Association of Leadership Educators.

ABOUT THE BOOK

Our interest in Generation Z students emerged while working together in a campus-based Leadership Programs office that housed a four-year comprehensive leadership program, a three-day national leadership conference, a yearlong multi-track leadership workshop series, a co-op program, and a minor in Leadership Studies and Practice.

Our story began during the summer of 2013 when we noticed a bit of a shift in the students who were attending our summer orientation program. After doing some initial research, we learned that we were in the midst of a generational shift—one from Millennial students to Generation Z students. We knew that in order to recruit these new students into our programs as well as ensure our offerings aligned with their needs and interests, we needed to learn more about their characteristics, perspectives, beliefs, and styles. Thus, we began our quest to understand Generation Z.

In 2016, we released *Generation Z Goes to College*, which offers an in-depth view of Generation Z in higher education and consists of findings from our *Generation Z Goes to College Study*, a quantitative and qualitative study of more than seven hundred Generation Z students from fifteen colleges and universities conducted during the first six weeks of college. In addition to our research, we included data from external studies, including findings derived from the dataset of more than 150,000 Generation Z students from the 2014 *CIRP Freshman Survey*.[1] We have since conducted the *Generation Z Stories Study*, which includes narratives from more than twelve hundred students across more than fifty higher education institutions in the United States and Canada. That study was designed to uncover the perspectives, motivations, aspirations, and concerns of members of this generation as they emerge into adulthood.

This book includes findings from our research and external studies that are specifically influential to Generation Z college student leadership development. In the chapters that follow, you will find information about barriers to engagement and value propositions that align with Generation Z, marketing and recruitment strategies, approaches for structuring and designing training and development experiences, ideas for broadening the notion of service learning and volunteerism, guidelines for advising, as well as assessment and recognition practices.

INTRODUCTION

Since its inception, higher education has been a living, breathing entity that has adapted to the changing demographics of students. Now that higher education finally has a grasp on how to engage and educate Millennial students, a vastly different cohort has entered college with its own needs, aspirations, styles, and preferences. Meet Generation Z, born 1995–2010. The oldest ones graduated from college in 2017, but their presence continues to permeate higher education, as they will be our traditional-aged students through 2032.

Generation Z students identify as compassionate, loyal, responsible, and thoughtful.[2] They are committed to social change and social justice and seek education as a way to build their skills for the future. Being money conscious, tech savvy, and entrepreneurial,[3] finding ways to engage these students in leadership experiences will call for an approach different from what may have worked with previous generations.

1

ENGAGING GENERATION Z STUDENTS IN LEADERSHIP EXPERIENCES

A study by the National Association of Colleges and Employers found that nearly 70 percent of employers want to hire college graduates who have leadership skills.[4] Thus, it is no surprise that there are more than fifteen hundred college-leadership programs nationwide,[5] and nearly every college campus offers student organizations and co-curricular programming, with some even offering for-credit academic leadership programs. Despite the variance between campuses, for the purposes of this book, leadership experiences refer to leadership programs, events, trainings, and courses; student organizations; student government; recreational, social, and educational events and co-curricular programming; and any other experiences designed for college students to foster leadership development.

Barriers to Engagement

Despite the many opportunities to engage in a leadership experience, many Generation Z students may not have the ability or interest to participate. Factors such as cost, time, and perspectives on leadership may influence their involvement.

Cost of Engagement

With college tuition having risen more than 80 percent between 2003 and 2013,[6] many students need to take on massive student loan debt to attend college, resulting in an average of $34,000 of debt per student.[7] It is no surprise then that we found through our *Generation Z Goes to College Study* that more Generation Z students are concerned about the cost of college than any other issue, with more than half indicating being "very concerned."[8] One student in our *Generation Z Goes to College Study* sums up the general sentiment of our participants in saying, "Even a college degree can no longer guarantee a job, making me wonder if spending thousands of dollars on a degree is going to be worth it."[9]

Because student loan debt is negatively related to persistence,[10] it would not be surprising if some Generation Z students determine partway through college that accruing vast amounts of debt is not in their best interest and end up leaving college. For students who end up persisting until graduation, some may opt out of participating in programs and organizations that have associated fees to participate, not wanting to add to the insurmountable debt they are accruing. Not only do they not want to pay extra for programs and services, a majority believe that having fewer programs and services offered on campus could help reduce costs for higher education.[11] For students who may not even be interested in paying a library fee or recreation center fee, it might be a hard sell to elicit their participation in fee-based leadership experiences. Thus, it is critical for those leadership programs that need fee-based revenue for operations to articulate the value of participation.

Time for Engagement

With the growing number of students who need to work while in college to offset expenses,[12] there may be little time left to participate in leadership experiences. In trying to choose between picking up more shifts at work for the weekend and going on a leadership retreat, it can seem like an obvious decision for those students who need the money to offset their tuition, living expenses, or student loan debt. In addition, with the high cost of higher education, some students may take excessive course loads to earn their degree in a shorter amount of time. More classes and more studying may mean less time for leadership experiences. With less time to participate, this generation of students is likely going to be far more critical about how they spend the little free time they have, impacting their desire to commit long term to an organization, role, or program.

Perspectives on Leadership

It may be more than just the time and cost of involvement that may impede the participation of Generation Z students in leadership experiences. Their dislike for formal, positional leadership may shape their perspectives of wanting to be a leader. According to Northeastern University's *Innovation Survey*, political leaders were found to be the least likely number-one role model for Generation Z.[13] This is no surprise given that many Generation Z students believe that politicians are dishonest, selfish, and argumentative.[14] One Generation Z student in our *Generation Z Goes to College Study,* when discussing political leaders, said, "Dysfunctional leaders tend to result in a dysfunctional country."[15] How members of Generation Z see traditional positional leaders may influence the extent to which they aspire to be positional leaders themselves, now or in the future. It might not be surprising then to see Generation Z students being reluctant about holding student organization executive roles, participating in student government, or engaging in leadership development programs or courses.

Their perspective on leadership provides both a challenge and an opportunity. First, with the world structured around formal leadership positions, it is important to help Generation Z students understand that positional leadership is not necessarily the problem, yet it may be more of an issue of the unethical and corrupt behaviors of those who occupy those roles. On the other side, their cautionary view of positional leadership might offer an opportunity to highlight the value of nonpositional leadership as being an influential and positive form of leadership. Because Generation Z students see those closest to them as role models,[16] there might be a unique opportunity to associate behaviors that provide positive role modeling as leadership, even without a formal position.

In addition to their view of others as leaders, Generation Z students have a potentially inflated sense of their own leadership ability. Nearly 63 percent of more than 150,000 Generation Z students in the 2014 *CIRP Freshman Survey*[17] rated their leadership ability either above average or in the highest 10 percent. In one sense, they see leadership as negative when practiced by many positional leaders, yet in another, they see themselves being extremely proficient in it.

Why Get Involved? Value Propositions for Generation Z

Given the potential time and cost of participation and Generation Z students' leeriness of leadership in general, drawing Generation Z students into leadership experiences may be challenging. Messages of joining a club or program because "it's fun" or "it will help you make friends" might not work with Generation Z students. Instead, consider incorporating specific value propositions into your recruitment messaging. Below are four critical value propositions for helping Generation Z students see the value of engaging in leadership experiences.

Develop into Ethical, Positive, and Caring Leaders

Generation Z students are bombarded with news updates and social media posts filled with examples of unethical and corrupt political, business, and community leaders. Their unfavorable view of leadership may be convincing enough for them to opt out of taking on leadership roles or participating in leadership experiences. But given that 69 percent of them indicated that their parents were their number-one role models,[18] the people closest to them might be the best examples of good leaders. It can be easy to be swept away by constant news of bad leadership and miss the many instances of ethical and positive leadership around them. Perhaps after realizing that not all leaders are bad, students may want to aspire to be *good* and *ethical* leaders themselves.

- **Value proposition:** Participating in leadership experiences, programs, or courses can provide you both the training and the space to discuss and practice ethical, positive, and caring leadership in a time in which this type of leadership is sorely needed.
- **Action:** In marketing and publicity efforts for leadership opportunities, highlight examples of positive leaders and discuss the need for ethical, positive, and caring leadership.

Develop Critical Career Competencies

Generation Z students are highly career-focused and see college as a way to develop the skills they need to be successful in the future. This is no different for their leadership experiences. One student in the *Generation Z Stories Study* commented, "I am involved in [a] leadership program at my school where we learn leadership skills and the necessary tools to lead effectively. I have already used these skills at work and school."[19] With employers valuing leadership competencies,[20] it is important to be able to articulate to students the competencies that they will be developing as a result of participating in particular leadership experiences. For example, if students understand that being the president of a student organization can help them develop particular leadership competencies such as fostering group development, facilitating meetings, and leading collaborative efforts, they may see the value that participating in this role may offer beyond simply listing the experience on their résumé. In addition, possessing a variety of leadership competencies that can be applied in multiple types of roles and experiences can serve students well as they transition in and out of different careers.

- **Value proposition:** Participating in leadership experiences can help you develop the competencies you need to be successful in the future.
- **Action:** Identify competencies associated with each leadership experience, role, program, event, and course offered. Help students select experiences based on the competencies they want to develop as well as articulate those competencies in their résumés, interviews, and so on.

Pursue Passions

Generation Z students are keenly aware that passion plays a huge role in their happiness.[21] As one student in our *Generation Z Stories Study* indicated, "A good life is one full of passion, laughter, and fulfillment. It is a life where I am passionate about everything I do."[22] Thus, it is no surprise that 75 percent of Generation Z students from our *Generation Z Goes to College Study* are motivated to action if it is tied to their passions.[23] These passion-driven students want to ensure that they use their very limited time and resources to pursue what they believe is their greater calling in life. This is not simply relegated to career choice, although that is significant for these students. Helping them find opportunities that fit with their passions is critical for involving these students in leadership experiences. For example, a student who cares deeply about recycling could be connected to an environmental organization, a programming board to set up environmental events, leadership roles in programs and offices across campus that focus on environmental work, or courses that focus on environmentalism.

- **Value proposition:** Participating in leadership experiences can help fuel your passions and can be a great way to get involved in something you love.
- **Action:** Consider setting up a searchable database of student organizations, roles, events, and programs related to different issues so students can easily search for experiences by their passion area (for example, social justice, environment, or technology). And if students cannot find opportunities

related to the issues they are passionate about, help them connect with organizations in the local community or create additional experiences on campus.

- **Action:** For academic courses, consider tagging community-based learning courses and designate them through the registrar. Then, students can search these types of classes to find ones that align with their passions.

Make a Difference

In our *Generation Z Stories Study*, students ranked making a difference as the second most important criteria in their future careers, ranked only after enjoying the work.[24] A student from the study sums up this sentiment in saying,

The most important thing to me in my future career is making a difference. I really want to help others and impact them for the better. Clearly, I will need to financially support myself, but that's not why my heart will be in it. If I get caught in the chase for that perfect American dream, then I'll waste the talents and gifts and time that I have. I would rather end my life knowing that I truly made a positive difference.[25]

This desire to make a difference is not just important for their careers. Seventy-five percent of students in our *Generation Z Goes to College Study* are motivated simply by knowing that what they are doing in any aspect of their lives is making a difference for someone else.[26] Their desire to make a difference aligns seamlessly with the purpose of many leadership experiences. Whether serving in student government and advocating for student needs, being a member of a student organization that plans events for others, participating in a community-based project in a leadership course, or being a resident assistant and helping ensure students are living in a safe, healthy, and supportive environment, participating in a leadership experience on campus can be synonymous with making a difference. But it might be hard for students to readily see their participation serving a larger purpose in making a difference for others.

- **Value proposition:** Participating in leadership experiences can help you connect with resources and networks to make a difference in the lives of others.
- **Action:** Help current student organization members and those who have participated in leadership programs, events, roles, and courses identify how they have made a difference in the lives of others and encourage them to communicate this to other students as a way to get them involved.

2

MARKETING AND RECRUITMENT

In order to enlist Generation Z students to participate in leadership experiences, it is critical to ensure that recruitment messaging aligns with the value propositions described earlier. Some students may resonate with one value proposition more than another, or a particular proposition might be more appropriate for what students are being recruited for. Once the messaging has been determined, it is important to consider strategies specifically designed to recruit Generation Z students.

Recruiting Generation Z Students

Although many existing strategies, such as providing give-aways or food, will likely work in recruiting this generation to participate in leadership experiences, there are some nuanced strategies that align specifically with the preferences of Generation Z students. These include using recruitment videos, targeted social media messaging, online polling, hashtags, group texting, face-to-face connection, parent and family marketing, and a refer-a-friend approach.

Recruitment Videos

As those in other generations might venture to Google to learn about new information, Generation Z students seek out YouTube specifically as a place for learning.[27] One Generation Z student from our study said, "I use YouTube because it has the most interesting content."[28] They are not inclined to read e-mails[29] and may not see a flyer or poster, so short videos may be the way to get information out about student organizations, leadership programs, service opportunities, leadership courses, and leadership roles. In putting together a video, it is important that:

- Those in the video are students, and the video is narrated by students.

- The video is between two minutes and six minutes. After six minutes, you will likely lose their attention.
- The content is interesting and showcases hands-on engagement and not simply people giving testimonials. Make sure to include examples of the value propositions in action.

Social Media Messaging

It may be easy to assume that Generation Z students are always on social media posting information about every thought or action they experience. However, in our *Generation Z Goes to College Study*, we found that while more than 80 percent of students use Facebook to keep up with others, only 54 percent use the platform to post about themselves.[30] Their reluctance in posting reflects their hesitance in sharing details about themselves with everyone in the digital world.[31] Because of this, they are likely not to want offices, programs, or educators themselves connecting with them on their personal social media accounts, although they may be more okay with joining an organization's Facebook group or connecting through a platform that they don't readily post to with friends. This differs drastically from Millennials, who appear to use Facebook as the central hub for everything, combining their personal, professional, and educational connections into one virtual space. Because of their strategic social media use in using different platforms for specific reasons,[32] it may be helpful to select a platform to use for your office or program that Generation Z students use while making sure not to enter their most private virtual space. For example, having an Instagram account to post photos, updates, and opportunities could reach this population well without encroaching on their personal space on another platform such as Snapchat.

In addition, when using Instagram, instead of posting only announcements, make their involvement with the account interactive. Add a video or picture with a question or clue to a puzzle that can only be answered at the upcoming event. The key is to make sure that the social media post requires action on their part—click a link, watch a video, or post a response. Also, encourage students to post and share photos on the office or program Instagram site (pending their appropriateness). By engaging them before the event, Generation Z students might be more motivated to show up to the actual event.

Another social media platform that may be useful for connecting with Generation Z is Twitter due to the ability to share quick announcements and updates. Not only is it easy to use, Twitter can reach a broad audience, which is why it is no surprise that it is the social media platform of choice for student affairs administrators to communicate with students.[33] Although some Generation Z students use Twitter to share information specifically with their friends, more than three-quarters use it to keep up with others.[34]

Knowing that they like to follow Twitter and that they are aware that professionals are in that virtual space, Twitter may offer a universal social media space for both students and educators to occupy. Regardless of platform used, it is important to make sure to not over-post on social media, as this can lead to students not paying attention to posts or unfollowing social media accounts altogether.

Online Polling

Another recruitment strategy is to post links to online polls and surveys in your marketing materials and social media messaging so students can give their opinions before the event or experience. It may be that students get to vote on which nonprofit to donate funds to for the philanthropy, what color T-shirts to order, or what topic the class should focus on for the group project. Or it may be fun trivia leading up to the event in which students can cast their votes. Online polling can not only provide great feedback before an event or program but also can serve as a way to create a vested interest with the students in the outcome of the poll and ultimately the program or event.

Hashtags

Using hashtags in digital communication is a strategic way to expand marketing efforts. Consider having a program-specific or institution-specific hashtag that accompanies all of your programs or events such as #stateuleadership. Using hashtags offers the opportunity to elicit a buzz around an upcoming event or chatter around news. Encourage students to use the hashtag as well as to track the hashtag on their social media accounts.

Group Texting

As Generation Z students use text messaging frequently,[35] sending periodic text announcements is a great way to market and recruit these students. One option is to have students subscribe to a site such as Remind 101 where they can get updates about leadership opportunities sent directly to their phones as text messages. Students control their subscriptions and do not need to provide phone numbers to the institution directly, allowing them to opt out at any time. Like social media, be mindful of the number and frequency of texts and reminders. Too many might drive away students.

Face-to-Face Connection

Although they appear buried in their phones, Generation Z students actually prefer in-person human interaction to all other forms of communication.[36] It can be helpful to ask instructors, mentors, advisors, and others who have existing relationships with students to shoulder tap those they personally know to participate in leadership experiences. Because these individuals likely know the students better than others at the institution, they can leverage particular value propositions specific to each student to personalize their recruitment efforts.

Parent Marketing

Because Generation Z students seek advice from their parents who are their most trusted mentors,[37] marketing to parents is essential. Unlike parents of Millennials who were more like helicopter parents, hovering uninvited over their students, Generation Z students see their parents as copilots in their decision-making.[38] If the parent of a Generation Z student believes a leadership experience is beneficial, the student may as well. Although Generation Z students might not be on Facebook as much as they are on other platforms,[39] their parents often are. Have parents subscribe through their social media accounts and then craft messages specific to them that they can communicate with their students.

Refer-a-Friend

Peers play a prominent role in influencing Generation Z's decision-making.[40] They can influence what products to buy, what college to attend, or even what leadership opportunities to participate in. Because of this, peer recruitment may be an excellent strategy to employ to recruit students for leadership experiences. There is no better advocate for joining a club, going to an event, or participating in a program or course than students who are actively involved. At the most basic level, utilizing peer influence means having student ambassadors engaging in recruiting efforts or students presenting information sessions. However, to take this to the next level, it is critical to leverage the relationships that students have with each other in recommending leadership experiences. One such way to do this is through a Refer-a-Friend program.[41] This approach involves asking students who are already involved to bring one friend to the next meeting or event to try out the leadership experience. Even having students in a leadership course bring a friend to their final presentation can pique the interest of those friends to take the class in the future. Using the Refer-a-Friend approach can increase attendance while capitalizing on the legitimacy that the involved students possess with their peers.

3

CONTENT

As discussed in chapter one, Generation Z students want to be assured that the time, energy, and money they spend on something is an investment in their future. Therefore, it is important to be able to incorporate into the leadership curriculum both what Generation Z students will need in order to successfully practice leadership along with what they actually want to learn. To do so, there are two areas of focus to consider when embedding leadership content into a program, event, course, or role. These include infusing essential leadership competencies and fostering social justice.

Infusing Essential Leadership Competencies

Because of the vast amount of content that could be considered "leadership," it might be difficult to identify specific competencies critical for Generation Z students. Understanding the context of today's pressing leadership challenges and the values of Generation Z students can help educators in the selection of specific competencies to incorporate into leadership experiences.

Complexity

The definition of leadership has changed through the years based on the context of society at the time, along with the perspectives of those living in it.[42] Today is no different as there is a need for leadership that will address the many complex problems facing the world today and in the future. In *Generation Z Goes to College*, we discussed nine specific competency areas that Generation Z students may benefit from developing based on both their perspectives of leadership as well as what may be necessary to address complex challenges. These include the following:

- Leveraging the capacity of others
- Engaging in complex thinking and innovative problem solving

- Utilizing a collaborative and interdependent approach
- Communicating effectively
- Being adaptable
- Guiding others to greatness
- Being optimistic
- Persevering through adversity
- Employing honesty and altruism

Incorporating these competency areas into the curriculum or the duties of a leadership role can help prepare Generation Z students for the many complex leadership challenges ahead.

Career Competencies

The National Association of Colleges and Employers provides a list of competencies that employers look for in college graduates, which could also greatly inform leadership content development. These most sought after competencies include the ability to work in a team, problem-solving skills, written communication skills, strong work ethic, and verbal communication skills.[43] Verbal communication and writing were also found to be among the three most prevalent competencies required for graduates across all 522 accredited academic programs in the United States, in addition to the competency of evaluation.[44] All of these competencies are not only important to integrate into the curriculum from a career preparation standpoint, but also, as discussed earlier, doing so might lure career-minded Generation Z students to participate.

Holistic Competency Development

Regardless of the competency to be developed, it will be important to engage Generation Z students in a holistic approach that focuses on developing the knowledge, value, ability, and behavior dimensions of each competency.[45] To help develop the knowledge dimension, consider offering opportunities for students to increase their foundational understanding of the competency through sharing of new ideas, strategies, models, and theories. For example, enhancing the knowledge dimension of the competency of adaptability might include offering opportunities for students to learn about strategies and best practices for being adaptable. For the value dimension, consider integrating components into the experience that help students see the value of the competency. For the example of adaptability, this might include sharing stories of motivation and inspiration that highlight the importance of being adaptable. For the ability dimension, consider offering experiences that allow students to develop their proficiency in using the competency. For example, a simulation that incorporates having to deal with some type of change would give students an opportunity to practice their adaptability. For the behavior dimension, consider providing experiences or roles in which students use the competency in a real-life setting such as being on a student government committee that has to adapt policies based on student feedback.

Fostering Social Justice

Generation Z students are the most racially diverse generation in modern history and have the most diverse social circles.[46] Enhanced exposure to differences along with their open-mindedness[47] have made diversity more of a norm than something to be tolerant or aware of, as was the focus with previous generations. Even Generation Z students who came from homogeneous geographic areas or lacked diverse interaction growing up have been exposed to people who are different from them through television and media. This normative exposure likely explains why many Generation Z students in our *Generation Z Stories Study* believe that the diversity of backgrounds, identities, perspectives, and experiences of people make the world a better place.[48]

Moving toward Social Justice

Whether woven into trainings, retreats, workshops, courses, or other programs and events, diversity has been a foundational element in many leadership experiences. Given Generation Z's substantial exposure to diversity, it may be time to shift these experiences more toward social justice than diversity awareness. Today's political climate has brought out an undercurrent of issues related to racism, sexism, heterosexism, xenophobia, religious oppression, transphobia, and the like, meaning that there is no better time to help our students learn about and practice social justice. This recommended shift toward social justice aligns with findings from our *Generation Z Stories Study* in which students expressed an inclusive attitude and commitment to social justice.[49] Our earlier *Generation Z Goes to College Study* also found that many Generation Z students are concerned about racial equality, limitations on personal freedom, human rights, sexism, and economic inequality.[50] Although it is important not to abandon diversity awareness programs that help students understand identities they are less familiar with, moving programming and experiences toward a social justice frame can be beneficial for this generation. First, social justice is about action and not simply awareness, which resonates with this social change-minded generation.[51] Second, social justice offers a way for Generation Z students to engage in actions around issues they are concerned about. Finally, social justice work gives students the opportunity to participate in a different form of leadership that might challenge their negative perceptions surrounding positional leaders.

Social Justice Leadership

Although many Generation Z students believe in social justice, they do not necessarily engage in social justice practices.[52] Many stay informed and share news of pertinent social issues with others, but fewer vote, campaign for candidates, or engage in lifestyle choices that support causes they care about. And, even fewer participate in advocating or protesting.[53] What this may mean is that social justice experiences may need to focus less on why social justice is important and more on how to actually develop the competencies needed to engage in actions and behaviors that contribute to social justice leadership.

4

ORGANIZATION AND PROGRAM DESIGN

Regardless of how good the marketing and recruitment strategies are, if what Generation Z students are being recruited for does not align with their interests and needs, they may not participate anyway. Thus, it is important to ensure that organizational and programmatic structures appeal to Generation Z.

Structuring Experiences

Ideas for re-conceptualizing traditional leadership experiences may include integrating outcomes from the co-curriculum into credit-based experiences, focusing on leadership development rather than leader development, infusing elements of gamification, rethinking positional leadership titles, and creating more opportunities for short-term involvement.

Credit-Based Experiences

Given that Generation Z students may lack the time or money to participate in leadership experiences, integrating the outcomes traditionally associated with co-curricular experiences into the credit-based curriculum may cast a wider net for participation. Students could take a leadership class in place of another elective or as a general education course, freeing up time for participation and rolling fees into their overall tuition.

Another way to offer academic credit for leadership experiences is by providing a hybrid leadership course in partnership between student affairs and academic affairs. The class could meet once a month with a faculty member to cover pertinent leadership content and then the time between class sessions can be used for team projects and community-based learning coordinated by a student affairs administrator.

In addition, having students earn academic credit for participation in learning experiences such as a multiday social justice retreat or civic engagement conference could expand participation. The credits earned from these experiences could count in students' overall course loads, freeing up time for them to participate because they would have one less class to take during the semester. In addition, with the ability to add course fees, units offering these experiences could recoup costs associated with the activity that can be paid for by students using financial aid. And students who are interested in moving more quickly toward graduation may want to add these types of courses to an already full load because the nature of the subject matter or time offered may fit with an already busy schedule.

Another way to incorporate credit-based leadership opportunities is by allowing students to use a leadership experience to satisfy an internship requirement if the role meets the learning objectives of the academic department. Critical career competencies such as collaboration and verbal communication[54] are already embedded into many leadership experiences. With the demand for internships, it may be a win-win for institutions to re-conceptualize what an on-campus "leadership" internship might look like and how it can be mutually beneficial for both the students and the institution.

Offering credit hours for experiences that take place in the traditional co-curriculum may provide an innovative way to help students engage in meaningful learning that contributes to their college completion.

Gamification

Generation Z students are motivated by setting and completing benchmarks that culminate in the achievement of a larger goal.[55] This process of working toward one milestone at a time aligns with the notion of gamification in which experiences can be sequenced and scaffolded in a manner that encourages continued participation. Gamification involves using traditional game elements in nongame contexts as a way to motivate users.[56] Gamification can be digital, as seen in the use of various apps that award users with stars, badges, and rewards after completing certain tasks or levels. Gamification can also be applied in nondigital settings in which people can earn rewards for completion of particular tasks, such as getting a stamp on a new student orientation passport for visiting various campus offices. Students who have all stamps on their passport can enter to win a prize.

Implementing gaming elements into leadership experiences might create enough motivation for Generation Z students to get started on that first task or experience. Once completed, students may be motivated to complete yet another task or experience until they are ushered to the finish line. It is important to note, however, that Generation Z students do not like to individually compete with their peers,[57] so it is critical that any gamified experience is not set up as a race against others with scores posted for all to see. Instead, consider using a gaming mentality to either foster self-competition in which students try to achieve their own goals or set up formal group competitions, like a pitch or project competition, with rewards and recognition for the entire group.

Leadership versus Leader Development

Generation Z students' skeptical view of positional leadership may also influence their leadership behavior. When in groups, Generation Z students more often engage in executing a task (doing), fostering group development (relating), and thinking strategically (thinking) than leading a group (leading).[58] Although all of these behaviors may constitute some form of leadership, Generation Z students' lesser identification with the traditional act of leading, specifically, may be telling. Concepts like leading, lead, and leader may hold negative connotations with them. It may be time to reframe leadership programs and opportunities to be about developing leadership competencies and skills rather than about developing students into leaders.

Position Titles

Given that Generation Z students engage in leading less frequently than doing, relating, and thinking when in groups,[59] it may be time to reconsider the use of positional titles for leadership roles, especially in student organizations. Today, most institutions require student organizations to file paperwork each year that outlines specific details about the organization, including names associated with particular positions. For example, it is common that student organization paperwork asks for the name of a president, vice president, secretary, and treasurer. However, for a generation that needs a lot of convincing that leadership can be good and is witness to countless examples of bad positional leadership, it is not surprising that they may not be eager to sign on for a leadership position. If the purpose in requiring those specific position titles is to ensure the organization has a stable structure with a contact to the institution, that could be achieved by simply having students list four members of the organization and identifying the main contact person. A rigid hierarchical structure that involves defined positions may be unnecessary. If the students in a particular organization want to employ a hierarchical and positional structure, they could decide that for themselves. However, some students may want their organizations to employ rotating leadership, organic leadership, co-chairs, or simply an all-member organization. Allowing them to explore alternative organizational structures may be beneficial for them as well as open their eyes to new ways of engaging in leadership.

Engaging Underground Organizations

Having registered student organizations is certainly important, in that there is an official record of all organizations and a process for accountability at the institution. However, Generation Z students may not see many benefits in registering their organizations with the institution. With many venues available for gathering (for free), social media and apps for recruiting and organization management, and the often cumbersome institutional paperwork required to be a formal organization, there will likely be a growth in the number of "underground organizations" on campus. It is important to find a way for these organizations to come out of the shadows. Perhaps relieving some of the paperwork and hierarchical requirements of being a registered student organization may entice these clubs to register with the institution, thus not only providing them the many benefits awarded to registered groups but also limiting institutional liability.

Short-Term Involvement

Knowing that Generation Z students want to invest their time into what they are passionate about, they are likely not going to get involved on campus just to get involved. If students cannot find an organization that is a good fit, encourage them to form their own organizations, even if it means having five gaming groups and twelve hiking clubs.

Also, to capitalize on the success of Meetup.com, an online platform that brings people with similar interests together to "do, explore, teach, and learn the things that help them come alive,"[60] consider offering a campus-wide program that allows students to post institutionally approved events on an online bulletin board in an effort to gather with other students who share their interests. This allows students to engage in activities that have low commitment for continued involvement, unlike student organization membership, as well as focus around a very specific interest area (e.g., ballroom dancing or playing cards). The nature of these events is that they foster organic leadership. A student who wants to lead a hike just one time can post an event, lead the hike, and be done with that leadership role. These types of events create an environment in which there is both a leaderless and leaderful group opportunity. While any student can lead, students can also participate without ever having to lead. In addition, these types of events do not require a lot of paperwork (only to the extent the institution wants to set up an event-approval process) and can easily be integrated into an online events calendar at the institution.

Leadership Training and Development

Many campuses offer training and development sessions either for students to attend as a requirement to hold a leadership role or for any student to attend to develop knowledge and skills on a particular topic. Both of these types of sessions are often offered in person at a specific time. However, this generation of students, with their busy schedules, may opt out of participating in roles or experiences that require in-person sessions at a set time that in their minds could be done online. So, as much as they enjoy communicating in-person,[61] they do not always see their learning needing to take place face-to-face, especially if resources are in place to help guide them in engaging in successful intrapersonal learning.

Online Repository

In an effort to tap into their intrapersonal learning preference[62] while ensuring the content they access is credible, consider offering an online repository that includes many vetted resources on a variety of leadership topics for students to access. Students could get on the site at 3:00 a.m. and watch a video on leading effective meetings or engage in an online module about making ethical decisions. One student in our *Generation Z Goes to College Study* indicated preferring learning that involves having "many examples given, either stories or pictures that illustrate the point,"[63] emphasizing the value of having a resource repository available around the clock. The resources and links in the repository could be internally developed and/or could include external content such as links to TED Talks, iTunes University videos, podcasts, or simply informational websites. Having a repository offers a one-stop shop for students to find credible and useful resources without having to spend time sorting through countless websites and videos online. Although not all leadership content is best taught through a podcast, recorded webinar, or video presentation, task-oriented components of leadership, such as running a meeting or setting goals, might be ideal to offer in one of these formats and posted to an online repository.

Positional Leadership Training

Because of Generation Z students' learning preference for working independently and at their own pace,[64] it may be beneficial to look at alternative delivery methods for training students for specific campus roles. Consider integrating online trainings instead of in-person sessions and videos and podcasts rather than text resources. This can save both the student and institution time and money because no one has to be in attendance, and resources can be created once and made available to infinite numbers of students for an indefinite period of time. In addition, online training might be better for learning in that it offers an opportunity for students to get the content they need to be successful in their roles while eliminating the "firehose" approach that pushes too much content at them in a short amount of time. For example, some elements of student organization executive board training could be more self-paced and web-based. Delivery methods could include pre-recorded videos, podcasts, online quizzes, and voiceover slide shows that take students through content such as paperwork submission processes, risk-management guidelines, or branding requirements. Students could complete an online module or quiz with a minimum proficiency to ensure they received and understood the content presented. And by placing these training resources in the online repository discussed earlier, students may be enticed to explore other resources in the repository.

In addition, instead of having two weeks of in-person resident assistant training where each student affairs department speaks to the resident assistants for thirty minutes about their services, consider offering a MOOC, or massive open online course. Using a MOOC, students could learn about each office through an online module with a built-in quiz or assignment to ensure they have learned the information.

Our recommendation is not to move all training to be independent and online but to incorporate a flipped approach in which students learn critical information or task-based skills on their own first, such as through web-based training or a MOOC, and engage in hands-on, applied activities afterward.[65] This allows in-person time to focus on applying the content learned online or delving deeper into a subject matter less conducive to being offered virtually. Methods for face-to-face learning could include case studies, role-plays, simulations, debates, and discussions. A student in our study highlighted a preference for a flipped approach in pointing out ideal learning as "independently watching videos and do-ing hands-on projects."[66]

The flipped approach could be applied to a multitude of student training opportunities in which the students first learn important content related to their roles through self-directed learning and then spend face-to-face time in-teracting with others and applying the content. For exam-ple, before returning to campus, resident assistants could engage in a web-based training or MOOC that covers the services and resources of each office and then spend a couple hours after returning to campus getting a tour of these spaces and asking follow-up questions to the staff. This approach allows students to learn about the offices ahead of time and later physically visit each space and en-gage in face-to-face communication with the professionals who work there.

Aside from capitalizing on Generation Z students' de-sire for self-directed and independent pre-learning coupled with social learning afterward,[67] a flipped learning ap-proach might also appeal to returning student leaders who do not want to participate in duplicate training from prior years. Nearly 20 percent of Generation Z students in our *Generation Z Stories Study* indicated that what they enjoy most about learning is being able to gain new knowledge.[68]

Having various levels of self-directed pre-learning opportunities might provide a way for "returners" to engage in learning that adds to their knowledge base.

Leadership Development Sessions

Leadership training, on the one hand, is often focused on ensuring students can effectively execute the leadership behaviors necessary for their particular roles. Leadership development, on the other hand, is more focused on enhancing specific leadership competencies and skills such as those around communication, self-awareness, and interpersonal relationships. For students who are in leadership roles and required to attend leadership development sessions, participation is nearly guaranteed. But, Generation Z students who are not required to participate may not see the benefit in coming to a live session that in effect offers information that could be easily accessed from the web. This may lead them to opt out of participating in workshops, retreats, and other live developmental sessions if they primarily consist of one-way content dissemination or, as they see it, information they could get in a short online video on their own.

Like training for leadership roles, consider using the flipped learning approach with leadership development sessions. For example, instead of having a workshop on building a résumé, students could access the online repository that includes uploaded examples of effective résumés, links to videos about best practices in résumé development, and even voiceover videos that take students step-by-step through the résumé-building process. Once students have completed their résumés using these sources, they could then attend a résumé lab where they get peer, staff, and employer feedback on their résumés and even practice their networking skills. This flipped approach may entice Generation Z students to attend these labs knowing that they will be using the live time for interaction and feedback rather than simply to listen to the sage wisdom of the presenter.

5

VOLUNTEER EVENTS AND SERVICE LEARNING

Whether as a standalone office or program or as individual events offered through departments or organizations, community service is woven deeply into the fabric of higher education. In some cases, students are able to go to an actual volunteer office on campus or access a virtual office online to find service opportunities. In other cases, service experiences are built into leadership programs, programming boards, specific service-oriented organizations, or courses. But, the way that Generation Z students view service may challenge the systems and structures already in place on many campuses.

Moving from Service to Social Change

Although service can be reflective of taking on a long-term volunteer role in the community (serving on a board of directors or as a member of the Neighborhood Watch), working on an extended project (working with a nonprofit to build a community garden), or even committing to sustained involvement in a regular short-term experience (tutoring kids every week), the term "service" has come to be synonymous with engaging in a short-term project or initiative. The reality is that most service projects offered on college campuses are likely one-time or short-term experiences (semester-long) that can make an immediate impact but do not necessarily lead to sustainable change. For example, serving food at a local shelter can help people in the immediate sense but does very little to eradicate hunger or poverty. Because community needs are plentiful and many nonprofit organizations are under-resourced, this help is often welcome as well as easier to set up and ask students to commit to than long-term projects.

Short-term projects also aligned well with service-minded Millennial students who were drawn to experiences that focused heavily on the symptoms of a problem rather than the problem itself.[69] Unlike Millennials, though, Generation Z students are driven by the need to participate in experiences that promote sustainable, social change aimed to eradicate the underlying problem. This may stem from the vast amount of information that is now posted online drawing attention to various social issues. A student in our *Generation Z Stories Study* reflects the feelings of many Generation Z students in saying, "We need to focus on potential long-term issues and solve them rather than try to fix short-term problems now."[70]

Because of Generation Z's views on social change, we propose considering broadening the definition of and opportunities for service to include more social change-oriented activities or those that address underlying problems rather than symptoms. Ideas could include having students explore a social issue (hunger, literacy, racism, etc.) and engaging in action research, entrepreneurship, or social innovation to address that issue.

Action Research

Because of the vast amount of content available on the Internet, Generation Z students are exposed to more information than any other generation was when they were in college. With information being plentiful and accessible, action research offers a viable service option for Generation Z students. Action research is the process of engaging in "evaluative, investigative, and analytical research methods designed to diagnose problems or weaknesses...[and] develop practical solutions to address them quickly and efficiently."[71] To use an action research approach, have students research strategies for addressing a selected social issue. This may include researching best practices, promising programs, or data to support policy initiatives. Being able to come up with possible solutions to a problem could allow students the opportunity to advance the knowledge base that could ultimately address the underlying problem. For example, students could research how institutions maintain high student retention rates and then offer ideas for best practices to administrators at their own institutions. In addition to making a difference, the process of action research also aligns pedagogically with how Generation Z students like to learn. They want practical, applied learning experiences that are tied to what they care about.[72]

Action research experiences could be offered as a group effort in which each person researches a different element of the issue. Or students could participate in a case competition where teams compete by presenting their ideas to stakeholder community members who then select a winning team.

Entrepreneurship

Because nearly 50 percent of those in Generation Z want to work for themselves,[73] giving them opportunities to engage in entrepreneurship while in college can provide a way for them to give back to their communities while helping them develop the skills they need for their future careers. This is especially important as we continue in the gig economy.[74]

Many students, regardless of major, may actually end up working for themselves. This may be the graphic design major who engages in freelance work or the information technology major who contracts work with multiple organizations at a time.

It is no surprise then that nearly two-thirds believe that higher education should offer opportunities for students to learn basic business skills.[75] But not all students want to major or minor in business in order to learn these skills. It might be more suitable for students to earn a degree in their specialty area and take one or two courses on basic business foundations. With business classes on some campuses being restricted to those majoring or minoring in business, campuses have a great opportunity to offer co-curricular opportunities or a general education course that helps aspiring entrepreneurs. Consider having students compete for start-up funding to create a small business that addresses a campus issue or having them work with community funders to start up a business that addresses a community issue. For example, developing a youth center in a neighborhood with high truancy rates might help keep kids engaged in productive activities and reduce delinquent behavior. Offering entrepreneurship opportunities to students as a form of leadership development might necessitate a partnership or training from others on campus who specialize in entrepreneurship, paving the way for more integrated leadership opportunities that cut across academic and student affairs.

Social Innovation

Nearly 40 percent of Generation Z students plan to invent something that will make a difference in the world.[76] Being able to channel this inventive spirit can be useful in solving social issues. Students can work to develop new processes, programs, products, or technology aimed to address a problem. For example, students could develop a fitness app that helps reduce obesity or a new application process on campus that is more first-generation student friendly. Campuses could offer innovation days or hackathons in which student teams work together during a timed session to create a new innovation that addresses a specific issue. And leadership classes that integrate service learning could expand student opportunities to include social innovation as a means for completing course requirements.

Connecting Passion and Service

Generation Z students are motivated when they are passionate about the task or role they have undertaken.[77] Posting a flyer about a pre-planned service project might not motivate students to participate unless it happens to be on a topic they deeply care about. Because students likely will not participate in a service experience if they do not feel passionate about the issue, it might be important to survey them ahead of time on the issues they care most about and then plan events around those topics. In addition, being able to connect students to existing service opportunities that align with their passions might help with both their initial participation and sustained engagement.

Some students, however, might either not know what they are passionate about or think they have a passion for something they later discover they do not have. To help them explore their passions, consider offering a day of service in which students can participate in multiple types of opportunities connected to various issues. Doing so gives students the opportunity to learn about what they might be passionate about while confirming for others if they do indeed have the passion they thought they did.

6

ADVISING

Given the many differences between Generation Z students and preceding generations, it is no surprise that this generational cohort has unique needs and interests regarding being advised, whether one-on-one or in a group. Important elements of advising to consider include filling the role of a mentor, communicating effectively with Generation Z students, and providing guidance for professional development.

Mentoring

Generation Z students do not look to political leaders, athletes, or celebrities as their role models; the inspirational and motivating individuals in their lives are part of their inner circles.[78] Because parents are Generation Z's number-one role models,[79] students may seek to fill the void of parental mentorship and guidance while in college with a trusted adult on campus. This may be no different in that there have always been students who seek out the advice and guidance from campus professionals. However, many in Generation Z may be looking for a parental proxy—someone to stand in for their parents in the role of a trusted life mentor, reflecting the need for deep and authentic connection and not just advice. As you engage in these mentoring relationships, it will be important to have transparency and authenticity with students. Although it will be critical to maintain professional boundaries, having students get to know you may help build the bond that fosters effective mentoring.

Communicating Effectively

More Generation Z students prefer face-to-face communication than talking on the phone, e-mailing, or texting.[80] In addition to in-person communication, they also see communicating face-to-face through a virtual video platform such as Skype as being effective. One student in our *Generation Z Goes to College Study* pointed out liking "Skype because I can talk to people face to face (virtually) and share information or experiences even if they aren't physically there."[81] Thus, there may be a value in having in-person as well as virtual office hours so that students can interact with a professional face-to-face using either medium.

After face-to-face communication, Generation Z students' preferred communication method is text messaging.[82] They like one-on-one texting for quick questions and reminders, and using apps like GroupMe or Kik for group discussions and announcements may be a good way to stay connected to them. Although using text as the only form of advising is not recommended, texting can provide a useful way to engage with students for quick information exchange or time-sensitive discussions.

On the other hand, Generation Z students have very low preferences for using e-mail or phone to communicate with others.[83] One student in our *Generation Z Goes to College Study* commented, "I usually prefer to talk in person with someone because you can better connect with whoever you are talking to. You can't read facial/body expressions through a phone or e-mail but only with the human interaction."[84] Thus, it may be no surprise that some Generation Z students may go weeks or months without checking their campus e-mail account and rarely leave voicemails on office phones.

Although social media platforms such as Instagram and Twitter can be impactful for efforts to reach students for marketing, recruitment, and news updates, Generation

Z students might be more wary of using social media for one-on-one interaction with educators. First, given their limited posting to Facebook,[85] Generation Z students may end up eventually discontinuing their use of the platform altogether, including the group or organization page. Their discontinuation may mean that messaging students through Facebook may ultimately become a communication tool of the past. And as Generation Z students move to other platforms, as they are doing now with Snapchat, for example, students may also end up later leaving those spaces because they do not necessarily want adults in their private social media space.[86] Although social media can offer a gateway to a captive audience, unless students invite you into their personal social media space for ongoing connection, it may be more useful to work with students through platforms they prefer, such as face-to-face communication and texting.

Professional Development

As discussed earlier, Generation Z students are very mindful about how they spend their time and money. They want their leadership experiences to help them develop critical skills for their future careers. One student in our *Generation Z Stories Study* noted what is most important for a future career by saying, "I'd like to use my skills and gifts to make a difference in the world one day."[87] This mentality lends itself to having advisors use one-on-one time with students to engage in intentional and professional skill development in addition to personal check-ins and role updates that typically happen during these meetings. Advisors can craft developmental competency-based learning plans specific to each student and use their meeting time together for competency goal setting and reflection. Advisors may want to follow an outline such as this to provide an intentional approach to one-on-one professional development:

1. Explore the student's passions and interests. What is the student's calling? If the student is unsure, advisors can ask probing questions, provide self-assessments, or ask the student to engage in learning activities to uncover interests and passions.

2. Help the student identify careers related to a specific passion area. If the student already has a future career in mind, help connect the student's passions with the identified career.

3. Have the student research the identified career and explore essential competencies required of individuals working in that profession.

4. Have the student select one competency to develop related to the identified career.

5. Help the student articulate a measurable goal around the selected competency.

6. Refer the student to specific experiences to enhance the selected competency. These experiences may include attending training opportunities, adding responsibilities to the position, or taking on specific duties in the program/organization.

7. Have the student reflect on the progress of the goal, making enhancements and adjustments as necessary.

8. After each experience, help the student process any learning that occurred and set new goals.

Each of these steps can be woven into meeting times and discussed among many other critical agenda items. However, the continued revisiting of this practice will ensure that students have an intentional and developmental process to guide their professional development.

7

ASSESSING, SHOWCASING, AND RECOGNIZING ACHIEVEMENTS

With campuses offering a variety of leadership opportunities for students to choose from, it is important to uncover whether those experiences impact learning and development. Although assessing student leadership experiences is not a new phenomenon, working with Generation Z students offers an opportunity to consider innovative ways to collect data and help them showcase their learning.

Assessment

Much of the challenge in conducting assessment, aside from designing the instrument and protocol itself, is to engage in effective data collection methods that elicit enough and the right kind of data. Just like with other students, very few Generation Z students will want to take the time to complete a lengthy assessment. So it is important to identify which experiences will have more in-depth assessments associated with them and which ones will offer snapshot data like the examples offered below.

With Generation Z students' comfort with technology, integrating assessment into the digital experience can be a draw for these students. Consider using online surveys that are linked with a mobile-friendly URL. In addition, data collection can involve creative methods such as having students vote in an online phone poll, upload a picture to Instagram with a caption that sums up their learning from an experience, or text a response to a prompt. These methods may not bring in comprehensive data but can provide a means to get quick snapshot data from a large number of individuals.

Collecting data, however, can also be an organic process rather than one that is planned. For example, if there is a live feed to social media (Instagram or Twitter, for example) during an event, Generation Z students will likely be posting their thoughts throughout the time they are there. Looking for themes among the posts can provide great insight that can be used for assessment purposes.

Showcasing Achievements

Because Generation Z students want something to show for their participation, it is important to offer structured opportunities for them to showcase their learning. Three methods including digital badging, co-curricular transcripts, and electronic portfolios are described in further detail.

Digital Badging

Digital badges are electronic icons that are awarded to a user for the completion of a task or demonstration of learning, similar to what the Scouts have been doing for decades with physical badges. With leadership experiences, a badge could be awarded for holding a particular position, attending an event, or engaging in a project. Badges can be separated into categories such as service learning, leadership roles, and career development so that earning all badges in one category could result in the earning of the overall category badge.

But because Generation Z students are concerned about capitalizing on skill development during college,[88] it may be more useful for them to structure badging around competencies rather than experiences. Educators are able to decide the competencies associated with each leadership experience based on what the experience entails. Various experiences may have the same competency associated because the badge is about learning and not about the experience itself. For example, a student may participate in an alternative breaks trip that incorporates a service project and earn a competency badge on *social responsibility*, whereas another may earn the same badge by participating in an action research case competition. Students can accumulate their competency badges and display them on social media, electronic portfolios, or co-curricular transcripts to document their learning.

When infusing badging into a program or experience, it is important not to frame the earning of a badge as mastery of a competency, though. The badge serves as a reflection of the learning experience and not the proficiency level of the student who participated. In addition to showcasing learning, educators may be able to use data derived from tracking badge awards to capture information about competency development for individuals or groups of students uncovering themes related to student learning.

Co-Curricular Transcripts

Co-curricular transcripts are institutionally issued, verified documents of a student's co-curricular participation while in college. Like an academic transcript, students are able to showcase their leadership experiences with an official document beyond their self-reported résumé. Students can log their leadership roles, event participation, organization membership, and service learning, along with other categories selected by the institution. Upon completing an experience, the student is given credit by an official verifier who ensures the student participated. Some co-curricular transcripts have the option of including learning outcomes or competencies to demonstrate the learning associated with each experience. Because Generation Z students want to see concrete results from their involvement, a co-curricular transcript can serve as a culminating document that highlights their learning and development.

Electronic Portfolios

An electronic portfolio offers a digital space for students to collect and showcase their learning through a personalized website. With many open-source and organization management system platforms available, students can choose their design, layout, and privacy settings to customize their portfolio. They can include badges, certificates, co-curricular transcripts, sample work, photos, a résumé, and other tangible documents of their own content such as vision or destiny statements, goals, experiences, reflections, and competencies learned. Like co-curricular transcripts, electronic portfolios offer a way for Generation Z students to see the value of their leadership experiences in one space. The portfolio, however, does not just offer an end product for students. The process of developing the portfolio over time can serve as a way for Generation Z students to measure their progress toward milestones.

Recognition

Like other aspects of their leadership experiences, Generation Z students also have preferences for how they do and do not like to be recognized. For instance, these students may not enjoy the big end-of-year award celebrations like those in previous generations did. Just slightly more than one-quarter of Generation Z students prefer public recognition, and nearly the same number do not like it at all.[89] Because of this overall lack of preference for public recognition, some students who are award recipients may not want to get recognized at a public ceremony. The half that does not mind doing so also does not prefer it. Shifting to a less public form of recognition might appeal more to Generation Z students. Given that, we offer three recommendations regarding recognizing Generation Z students. These include leveling up experiences, achieving milestones, and providing endorsements.

Leveling Up

Nearly three-quarters of Generation Z students are motivated by the opportunity for advancement,[90] which lends itself well to the idea of leveling up or increasing the experience as one completes requirements. For example, a student who completes a leadership course and ten hours of shadowing a campus tour guide could be eligible to level up to be a tour guide in training and then after the completion of ten supervised tours, level up to be a tour guide. By creating intentionally designed, scaffolded leadership experiences, students can feel recognized simply by advancing to the next level. Levels may be tied to roles, such as the tour guide example, or the completion of particular requirements that unlock experiences that students would not otherwise be able to access without being at a certain level. One such example might be that participating in a certain number of workshops unlocks the ability to attend a luncheon with a community leader. In these cases, recognition is directly tied to their achievements, and the reward is unlocking new experiences.

Achieving Milestones

Given that Generation Z students like milestones as a way to see their progress toward a larger achievement, it is no surprise that their preference for recognition aligns with completing stepping-stones. Students in our *Generation Z Stories Study* commented on how they feel recognized just in achieving progress toward their goals. One student noted, "Being a day closer to achieving my dreams gets me excited every day. The path that I am taking is a long, hard one, but I know I will be rewarded for my efforts."[91] Given this, consider having students use a goal-setting app that could help them develop and track the progress of their own milestones. Having students achieve personal milestones may not result in any type of recognition given to the student at an awards ceremony or even by another person. But providing a process for students to recognize their own achievements may have a more lasting effect with Generation Z.

Endorsements

Another form of recognition that could be useful for Generation Z students is providing LinkedIn endorsements for specific achievements. As nearly 75 percent of students in our *Generation Z Goes to College Study* indicated being motivated by the opportunity for advancement,[92] having endorsements on a professional social media site such as

LinkedIn could contribute to opportunities that ultimately lead to future advancement. In addition, 68 percent noted seeing the fruits of their labor as being a strong motivator,[93] and having an endorsement may provide a symbolic indication of that labor.

Although these ideas might not feel like traditional recognition strategies, Generation Z students may find that these align more with who they are than being a recipient of the fanfare that public recognition often entails.

CONCLUSION

Decades of research indicate that leadership experiences are highly beneficial for students.[94] However, how these experiences have been structured and delivered in the past might not fit with the unique set of characteristics, styles, and perspectives of Generation Z. Educators must be willing to explore new approaches and strategies to leverage the talents and unlock the potential of these students. If not, Generation Z students may bypass the many wonderful leadership experiences offered on campus to chart their own course.

NOTES

1. Eagan, K., Stolzenberg, E. B., Ramirez, J. J., Aragon, M. C., Suchard, M. R., & Hurtado, S. (2014). *The American freshman: National norms fall 2014 (CIRP freshman survey).* Los Angeles: Higher Education Research Institute.
2. Seemiller, C., & Grace, M. (2016). *Generation Z goes to college.* San Francisco: Jossey-Bass.
3. Seemiller & Grace. (2016).
4. National Association of Colleges and Employers. (2016). *Job Outlook Survey.* Retrieved from http://www.naceweb.org/s11182015/employers-look-for-in-new-hires.aspx
5. Owen, J. (2012). *Examining the design and delivery of collegiate student leadership development programs.* Retrieved from http://leadershipstudy.net/wp-content/uploads/2012/07/msl-is-publication-final.pdf
6. Kurtzleben, D. (2013, October 23). *CHARTS: Just how fast has college tuition grown? US*

News & World Report. Retrieved from http://www.usnews.com/news/articles/2013/10/23//charts--just-how-fast-has-college-tuition-grown

7. Federal Reserve Bank of New York. (2017). *2017 press briefing: Household borrowing, student debt trends and homeownership.* Retrieved from https://www.newyorkfed.org/press/pressbriefings/household-borrowing-student-loans-homeownership

8. Seemiller, C., & Grace, M. (2014). *Generation Z goes to college study.* Unpublished raw data.

9. Seemiller, C., & Grace, M. (2014).

10. Hossler, D., Ziskin, M. B., Gross, J. P. K., Kim, S., & Cekic, O. (2009). Student aid and its role in encouraging persistence. In J. C. Smart (Ed.), *Higher Education: Handbook of Theory and Research* (Vol. 24, pp. 389–425). New York: Springer.

11. Northeastern University. (2014). *Innovation Survey.* Retrieved from www.northeastern.edu/news/2014/11/innovation-imperative-meet-generation-z/

12. Carnevale, A. P., Smith, N., Melton, M. & Price, E. W. (2015). *Learning while earning: The new normal.* Georgetown University. Retrieved from https://cew.georgetown.edu/wp-content/uploads/Working-Learners-Report.pdf

13. Northeastern University. (2014).

14. Seemiller & Grace. (2016).

15. Seemiller & Grace. (2014).

16. Seemiller & Grace. (2016).
17. Eagan, K., Stolzenberg, E. B., Ramirez, J. J., Aragon, M. C., Suchard, M. R., & Hurtado, S. (2014). *The American freshman: National norms fall 2014 (CIRP freshman survey)*. Los Angeles: Higher Education Research Institute.
18. Northeastern University. (2014).
19. Seemiller, C., & Grace, M. (2017). *Generation Z stories study*. Unpublished raw data.
20. National Association of Colleges and Employers. (2016).
21. Seemiller & Grace. (2017).
22. Seemiller & Grace. (2017).
23. Seemiller & Grace. (2016).
24. Seemiller & Grace. (2017).
25. Seemiller & Grace. (2017).
26. Seemiller & Grace. (2016).
27. Seemiller & Grace. (2016).
28. Seemiller & Grace. (2014).
29. Seemiller & Grace. (2016).
30. Seemiller & Grace. (2016).
31. Seemiller & Grace. (2016).
32. Seemiller & Grace. (2016).
33. Ahlquist, J. (2016). The digital identity of student affairs professionals. *New Directions for Student Services, 155*, 29-46.
34. Seemiller & Grace. (2014).

35. Seemiller & Grace. (2016).

36. Seemiller & Grace. (2016).

37. Northeastern University. (2014).

38. Seemiller & Grace. (2016).

39. Seemiller & Grace. (2016).

40. O'Leary, H. (2014). *Recruiting Gen Z: No more business as usual.* Retrieved from http://www.eduventures.com/2014/09/recruiting-gen-z/

41. Seemiller, C. (2014). *Enhancing student success through meaningful engagement opportunities.* OrgSync eBook.

42. Seemiller & Grace. (2016).

43. National Association of Colleges and Employers. (2016). *Job Outlook Survey.* Retrieved from http://www.naceweb.org/s11182015/employers-look-for-in-new-hires.aspx

44. Seemiller, C. (2013). *The student leadership competencies guidebook.* San Francisco: Jossey-Bass.

45. Seemiller, C. (2013).

46. Magid Generational Strategies. (2014). *The first generation of the twenty-first century: An introduction to the pluralist generation.* Retrieved from http://magid.com/sites/default/files/pdf/MagidPluralistGenerationWhitepaper.pdf

47. Seemiller & Grace. (2016).

48. Seemiller & Grace. (2017).

49. Seemiller & Grace. (2017).

50. Seemiller & Grace. (2014).

51. Seemiller & Grace. (2016).

52. Seemiller & Grace. (2014).

53. Seemiller & Grace. (2016).

54. National Association of Colleges and Employers. (2016).

55. Seemiller & Grace. (2016).

56. Deterding, S., Dixon, D., Khaled, R., & Nacke, L. (2011). From game design elements to gamefulness: Defining gamification. In *The ACM CHI Conference on Human Factors in Computing Systems 2011*, 12–15.

57. Seemiller & Grace. (2016).

58. Seemiller & Grace. (2016).

59. Seemiller & Grace. (2016).

60. Meetup.com. (2017). *About Meetup*. Retrieved from https://www.meetup.com/about/

61. Seemiller & Grace. (2016).

62. Seemiller & Grace. (2016).

63. Seemiller & Grace. (2014).

64. Seemiller & Grace. (2016).

65. Flipped Learning Network. (2014). *What is flipped learning?* Retrieved from https://flippedlearning.org/wp-content/uploads/2016/07/FLIP_handout_FNL_Web.pdf

66. Seemiller & Grace. (2014).

67. Seemiller & Grace. (2016).

68. Seemiller & Grace. (2017).

69. Lopez, M. H., Levine, P., Both, D., Kiesa, A., Kirby, E., & Marcelo, K. (2006). *The 2006 civic and political*

health of the nation. Retrieved from http://docplayer. net/12159697-The-2006-civic-and-political-health-of-the-nation-a-detailed-look-at-how-youth-participate-in-politics-and-communities.html

70. Seemiller & Grace. (2017).

71. Great Schools Partnership. (2015). *Action research.* Retrieved from http://edglossary.org/action-research/

72. Seemiller & Grace. (2017).

73. Sparks & Honey. (2014). *Meet Gen Z: Forget everything you learned about Millennials.* Retrieved from www.slide-share.net/sparksandhoney/generation-z-final-june-17

74. Upwork & Freelancers Union. (2016). *Freelancing in America: 2016.* Retrieved from https://www.upwork. com/press/2016/10/06/freelancing-in-america-2016/

75. Northeastern University. (2014).

76. Gallup & Operation Hope. (2013). *The 2013 Gallup-Hope Index.* Retrieved from www.operationhope.org/ images/uploads/Files/2013galluphopereport.pdf

77. Seemiller & Grace. (2016).

78. Seemiller & Grace. (2016).

79. Northeastern University. (2014).

80. Seemiller & Grace. (2016).

81. Seemiller & Grace. (2014).

82. Seemiller & Grace. (2016).

83. Seemiller & Grace. (2016).

84. Seemiller & Grace. (2014).

85. Seemiller & Grace. (2016).

86. Seemiller & Grace. (2016).
87. Seemiller & Grace. (2017).
88. Seemiller & Grace. (2016).
89. Seemiller & Grace. (2016).
90. Seemiller & Grace. (2016).
91. Seemiller & Grace. (2017).
92. Seemiller & Grace. (2016).
93. Seemiller & Grace. (2014).
94. Astin, A. W. (1999). Student involvement: A developmental theory for higher education. *Journal of College Student Development, 40*(5), 518–529.

REFERENCES

Ahlquist, J. (2016). The digital identity of student affairs professionals. *New Directions for Student Services, 155*, 29–46.

Astin, A. W. (1999). Student involvement: A developmental theory for higher education. *Journal of College Student Development, 40*(5), 518–529.

Carnevale, A. P., Smith, N., Melton, M., & Price, E. W. (2015). *Learning while earning: The new normal.* Georgetown University. Retrieved from https://cew.georgetown.edu/wp-content/uploads/Working-Learners-Report.pdf

Deterding, S., Dixon, D., Khaled, R., & Nacke, L. (2011). From game design elements to gamefulness: Defining gamification. In *The ACM CHI Conference on Human Factors in Computing Systems 2011*, 12–15.

Eagan, K., Stolzenberg, E. B., Ramirez, J. J., Aragon, M. C., Suchard, M. R., & Hurtado, S. (2014). *The*

American freshman: National norms fall 2014 (CIRP freshman survey). Los Angeles: Higher Education Research Institute.

Federal Reserve Bank of New York. (2017). *2017 press briefing: Household borrowing, student debt trends and homeownership.* Retrieved from https://www.newyorkfed.org/press/pressbriefings/household-borrowing-student-loans-homeownership

Flipped Learning Network. (2014). *What is flipped learning?* Retrieved from https://flippedlearning.org/wp-content/uploads/2016/07/FLIP_handout_FNL_Web.pdf

Gallup & Operation Hope. (2013). *The 2013 Gallup-Hope Index.* Retrieved from www.operationhope.org/images/uploads/Files/2013galluphopereport.pdf

Great Schools Partnership. (2015). *Action research.* Retrieved from http://edglossary.org/action-research/

Hossler, D., Ziskin, M. B., Gross, J. P. K., Kim, S., & Cekic, O. (2009). Student aid and its role in encouraging persistence. In J. C. Smart (Ed.), *Higher Education: Handbook of Theory and Research* (Vol. 24, pp. 389–425). New York: Springer.

Kurtzleben, D. (2013, October 23). *CHARTS: Just how fast has college tuition grown? US News & World Report.* Retrieved from http://www.usnews.com/news/articles/2013/10/23//charts--just-how-fast-has-college-tuition-grown

Lopez, M. H., Levine, P., Both, D., Kiesa, A., Kirby, E., & Marcelo, K. (2006). *The 2006 civic and political health of the nation*. Retrieved from http://docplayer. net/12159697-The-2006-civic-and-political-health-of-the-nation-a-detailed-look-at-how-youth-participate-in-politics-and-communities.html

Magid Generational Strategies. (2014). *The first generation of the twenty-first century: An introduction to the pluralist generation*. Retrieved from http://magid.com/sites/default/files/pdf/MagidPluralistGenerationWhitepaper.pdf

Meetup.com. (2017). *About Meetup*. Retrieved from https://www.meetup.com/about/

National Association of Colleges and Employers. (2016). *Job Outlook Survey*. Retrieved from http://www.naceweb.org/s11182015/employers-look-for-in-new-hires.aspx

Northeastern University. (2014). *Innovation Survey*. Retrieved from www.northeastern.edu/news/2014/11/innovation-imperative-meet-generation-z/

O'Leary, H. (2014). *Recruiting Gen Z: No more business as usual*. Retrieved from http://www.eduventures.com/2014/09/recruiting-gen-z/

Owen, J. (2012). *Examining the design and delivery of collegiate student leadership development programs*. Retrieved from http://leadershipstudy.net/wp-content/uploads/2012/07/msl-is-publication-final.pdf

Seemiller, C. (2014). *Enhancing student success through meaningful engagement opportunities*. OrgSync eBook.

Seemiller, C. (2013). *The student leadership competencies guidebook*. San Francisco: Jossey-Bass.

Seemiller, C., & Grace, M. (2017). *Generation Z stories study*. Unpublished raw data.

Seemiller, C., & Grace, M. (2016). *Generation Z goes to college*. San Francisco: Jossey-Bass.

Seemiller, C., & Grace, M. (2014). *Generation Z goes to college study*. Unpublished raw data. Sparks & Honey. (2014). *Meet Gen Z: Forget everything you learned about Millennials*. Retrieved from www.slideshare.net/sparksandhoney/generation-z-final-june-17

Upwork & Freelancers Union. (2016). *Freelancing in America: 2016*. Retrieved from https://www.upwork.com/press/2016/10/06/freelancing-in-america-2016/

INDEX